Strategic Studies Institute
and
U.S. Army War College Press

RUSSIAN MILITARY TRANSFORMATION – GOAL IN SIGHT?

Keir Giles
with
Andrew Monaghan

May 2014

*****

Comments pertaining to this report are invited and should be forwarded to: Director, Strategic Studies Institute and U.S. Army War College Press, U.S. Army War College, 47 Ashburn Drive, Carlisle, PA 17013-5010.

*****

This manuscript was funded by the U.S. Army War College External Research Associates Program. Information on this program is available on our website, *www.StrategicStudies Institute.army.mil*, at the Opportunities tab.

*****

The Strategic Studies Institute and U.S. Army War College Press publishes a monthly email newsletter to update the national security community on the research of our analysts, recent and forthcoming publications, and upcoming conferences sponsored by the Institute. Each newsletter also provides a strategic commentary by one of our research analysts. If you are interested in receiving this newsletter, please subscribe on the SSI website at *www.StrategicStudiesInstitute.army.mil/newsletter*.

FOREWORD

The questionable performance of the Russian armed forces in the conflict in Georgia in 2008 provided the impetus for a program of far-reaching reform in the Russian military. The progress of this reform has been the subject of intensive study, including in a number of monographs issued by the Strategic Studies Institute. But as Mr. Keir Giles and Dr. Andrew Monaghan describe in this Paper, the most recent phase of military transformation in Russia allows conclusions to be drawn about the final shape of the Russian military once the process is complete—and about the range of threats, some of them unrecognizable to us, that is guiding that process.

In this monograph, the authors use a wide range of Russian language sources and interviews to illustrate not only the Russian threat assessments highlighting the United States as a potential aggressor, but also the many unique challenges facing Russia in renewing and rearming its military. They conclude that, although many of the stated aims of reform will not be met, Russia will still have much more capable conventional and nuclear forces as a result. This, together with the Russian aim of closing the capability gap with the United States and the North Atlantic Treaty Organization, should be an essential consideration for U.S. decisionmakers evaluating options for reducing expenditure on the U.S. military capability.

This monograph was completed 6 months before the Russian military demonstrated its new capabilities in Crimea and Eastern Ukraine in early-2014. Presciently, the authors had concluded with a warning that close attention to Russian military transformation and its eventual aims was essential both for Russia's immediate neighbors, and for the United States. The Strategic Studies Institute therefore recommends this Letort Paper not only to scholars of Russia, but also to policymakers considering the range of challenges which the U.S. Army may be expected to face in the coming decades.

DOUGLAS C. LOVELACE, JR.
Director
Strategic Studies Institute and
    U.S. Army War College Press

ABOUT THE AUTHORS

KEIR GILES is the director of the Conflict Studies Research Centre (CSRC), a group of deep subject matter experts on Eurasian security formerly attached to the United Kingdom (UK) Ministry of Defence. Now operating in the private sector, CSRC provides in-depth analysis on a wide range of security issues affecting Russia and its relations with overseas partners. After beginning his career working with paramilitary aviation in Russia and Ukraine immediately following the fall of the Soviet Union, Mr. Giles joined the BBC Monitoring Service (BBCM) to report on political and military affairs in the former Soviet space. While attached from BBCM to CSRC at the UK Defence Academy, he wrote and briefed for UK and North Atlantic Treaty Organization government agencies on a wide range of Russian defense and security issues. Mr. Giles's work has appeared in a wide range of academic and military publications across Europe and in the United States. Uniquely, he is a double Associate Fellow of the Royal Institute of International Affairs (Chatham House) in London, UK, as well as a regular contributor to research projects on Russian security issues in both the UK and Europe.

ANDREW MONAGHAN is a Research Fellow in the Russia and Eurasia Programme at Chatham House and Academic Visitor at St Antony's College, Oxford United Kingdom (UK). He is the Founder and Director of the Russia Research Network, an independent organization for the generation of information and expertise on Russian politics, security, and economic issues, based in London. In this capacity, he has served as an expert witness to the House of Commons

Foreign Affairs Select Committee. Until late-2012, he directed Russian related research in the Research Division of the North Atlantic Treaty Organization's Defense College (NDC) located in Rome, Italy. In this role, he was also the NDC's senior researcher on energy security matters. Prior to that, he held positions as a Senior Research Associate at the Advanced Research and Assessment Group (ARAG), part of the Defence Academy of the UK, and a Visiting Lecturer in the Defence Studies Department of King's College, London, the civilian academic arm of the Joint Services Command and Staff College at the Defence Academy. Dr. Monaghan holds an M.A. in war studies and a Ph.D. in Russian foreign policy (Russian perspectives of Russia-EU security relations) from the Department of War Studies, King's College.

SUMMARY

The depth and scale of change that the Russian military has undergone during the last 5 years of transformation is impossible to overstate. This monograph reviews the overall direction and intention of Russia's military transformation, with particular reference to the specific range of threats—real and hypothetical—against which it is intended to ensure. Stated aspirations for transformation will be measured against known challenges facing the defense establishment and Russia as a whole, with the conclusion that several specific goals are unlikely to be met.

Fundamental organizational changes that finally broke the Russian armed forces away from the Soviet model in 2008-09 are now irreversible. It has been clear for some time that Russia no longer sees its military as a counter to a massive land incursion by a conventional enemy. While the idea of vulnerability to U.S. and North Atlantic Treaty Organization hostile intentions remains strong, this vulnerability finally is no longer seen in Cold War-era conventional military terms: instead, it is missile defense and precision strike capabilities that have come to the fore, even while lingering suspicions over a limited Libya-style intervention still provide a driving force for military modernization.

There is a persistent argument voiced by senior military commentators wielding prodigious authority in Russia that foreign powers are planning to seize Russia's natural resources, including by means of a paralyzing first strike by precision munitions against which Russia's air and space defenses will be entirely insufficient. This provides the backdrop for repeated statements by Vladimir Putin emphasizing defense against this eventuality. As a result, spending priorities and the transformation process overall are skewed and fail to address more realistic security threats to Russia. Spending on offensive strategic weapons has also been increased as a direct result of this consideration. One area that needs special consideration is Russian activity in developing and introducing new types of strategic weapons while continuing strengths in non-strategic nuclear weapons.

Meanwhile, the real and immediate security threat facing Russia is an entirely different one from an entirely different direction—Russia's southern periphery, where incursions, insurgency, weapons proliferation, and terrorism are all expected to increase in intensity following the U.S. and allied drawdown in Afghanistan and as a result of continued instability in the Middle East.

But many of Russia's remaining problems in implementing its transformation aims are not with money or equipment, but with people. Demographic change in Russia now means that service personnel are at a premium, and, for the first time in Russia's history, conscripts are a valuable asset rather than a disposable commodity. The examples of noncommissioned officer training and junior officer assignments show that Russia still awaits the fundamental cultural shift in how it treats its service people that is essential for dealing with human capital as a finite resource.

Deep and persistent challenges, including those of manning, funding, and procurement, mean that many ambitions for the Russian military will not be achieved in the short- to medium-term. All the same, it is undoubtedly the case that post-transformation Russia will have a very different force available from the one that went into action in Georgia in 2008, and one that is more effective, flexible, adaptable, and scalable for achieving Russia's foreign policy aims.

RUSSIAN MILITARY TRANSFORMATION—
GOAL IN SIGHT?

INTRODUCTION

The end of 2012 and beginning of 2013 brought apparently momentous changes for the Russian defense establishment. In addition to its recently-inaugurated new Commander-in-Chief, Vladimir Putin, the Russian military received a new Minister of Defence, Sergey Shoygu; a new Chief of General Staff, Valeriy Gerasimov; and a new Defense Plan in January 2013. Russian servicemen and defense commentators who had been highly critical of the main aims of military reform under the previous Minister, Anatoliy Serdyukov, were briefly optimistic that this could mean a reversal of some of its more controversial elements. But the statements and actions of the new leadership team to date suggest strongly that the direction of travel for Russia's military is now set, and reliable conclusions can now be drawn about its future.

This monograph seeks to review the overall direction and intention of Russia's military transformation, with particular reference to the specific range of threats—real and hypothetical—which it is intended to ensure against. Based on research up to September 2013, it reviews the period from 2011 when this transformation entered a qualitatively new and stable phase, which has continued through the change of leadership. It is not the intention to provide a detailed, blow-by-blow account of each reform initiative to date, since a number of excellent studies that do so are already available in both Russian and English.[1] But some of the stated aspirations for transformation will be measured against known challenges facing the

1

defense establishment and Russia as a whole, with the conclusion that several specific goals are unlikely to be met.

Fact and Fiction.

When examining the progress of Russia's military modernization, it is easy but dangerous to refer to public statements by senior Russian officials without measuring these statements against actual progress made or against reality. This monograph deliberately avoids citing statistics relating to reform plans. This is because despite the fact that many statistics from official Russian sources are widely quoted as indicative of what is actually happening in the Russian military, they are in almost all cases unreliable.

To illustrate this, we can use three key criteria and indicators of progress used by Russian officials to describe the reform process: "modern weapons," "readiness," and numbers of military personnel.

1. **"Modern Weapons."** A repeatedly stated key aim of military transformation and the accompanying rearmament spending is to increase the proportion of "modern" weapons and equipment in use in the Russian armed forces. There are aspirations to increase the specific percentage of equipment considered modern in different arms of service by specific dates. Yet nowhere has a reliable indicator been provided of what exactly "modern" means in this context—the word has been variously interpreted as meaning brand new, or under 10 years old, or recently renovated and upgraded. This lack of clarity gives the Russian armed forces considerable leeway in deciding when to declare that this criterion has been met, which at the same time means it cannot be used as a meaningful measure of progress.

2. **"Readiness."** Another key aim from the earliest stages of the transformation process was to increase the number of Russian military units which were at "permanent readiness." Yet again, there is no single overall definition for what precisely this means in a Russian military context. Common interpretations include defining readiness as being at a high state of manning or being actually combat-ready. Some Russian military officers suggest that being "ready" means being in a position to move rapidly away from the place of permanent basing in order to be outside a strike zone at the beginning of hostilities. In other words, "readiness" is purely a measure of force protection.[2] In any case, the lack of a commonly agreed definition limits the use of this metric as well.

3. **"Manpower."** It has been clear for almost a decade that the official figures for current numbers of servicemen, and plans for manning the armed forces in the future, are very remote from reality.[3] Yet Russian official sources persist in referring to a total manpower count of one million servicemen, despite mounting evidence that this is a purely notional and unachievable figure. Detailed discussion with senior Russians leads to a more nuanced and realistic picture, but the fact remains that it is impossible to deduce from open sources exactly what is Russia's military manpower strength.

This pattern continues throughout each statistical indicator describing the Russian military. As put by an authoritative Swedish study, "No single source on equipment holdings and the organization of Russia's Armed Forces is both verifiable and detailed enough to be useful to assess military capability."[4] For this reason, this monograph mostly avoids citing statistics and focuses instead on overall trends and verifiable events.

CHANGE AND CONTINUITY

The change in leadership for the Russian military brought some change in the direction of the armed forces that was real, and much more that was purely symbolic. It was signaled at an early stage that the fundamental organizational changes that have finally broken away from the Soviet model for the Russian armed forces are irreversible.[5] In a much-quoted speech, Putin told the Defence Ministry Board that:

> We cannot constantly chop and change. Once made, decisions must not be constantly changed. This is all the more important now that we have reached the stage of polishing and fine-tuning the many components in this complex military machine.[6]

This "polishing and fine-tuning" (*shlifovka*) has led to a number of top-level organizational changes that do not affect the overall structure of the armed forces. With a new law in late-December 2012, President Putin introduced important changes to the organizational structure of the armed forces, subordinating the General Staff directly to the President as Commander-in-Chief, as opposed to the previous system, where the Chief of General Staff reported to the Minister of Defence. In addition, the General Staff acquired new functions, which gave it direction of local authorities and organizations outside the Ministry of Defence for the purpose of organizing territorial defense.[7] This reversed the relative concentration of power in the person of the Minister of Defence that had been seen under Serdyukov.[8] This period also saw the creation of a

4

Russian Special Operations Command, which leading military analyst Dmitriy Trenin links to the incapacity of the Collective Security Treaty Organization (CSTO) Collective Rapid Reaction Forces, among other factors.[9] A new classified Defence Strategy through to 2016 was presented by Shoygu and Chief of General Staff (CGS) Gerasimov to President Putin in January 2013.[10] But by March 2013, 5 months after Shoygu reluctantly took office, an expert assessment was able to state that the main discernible difference was "a shift in favour of domestic military industry" from Serdyukov's attempts to promote the interests of the military as a customer, including through attempts to buy military equipment abroad.[11]

Many of the remaining apparent changes under Shoygu arguably can be described as purely symbolic and a sop to military pride. These include the Minister of Defence appearing in military uniform (although the practice of other officials appearing in uniform with rank badges corresponding to their civil service positions has received a mixed reception). Units have been granted historical names, and two high-prestige units have been restored from brigade to division status, even though at the time of writing, it remains to be seen whether this will translate into a full return to their previous composition.[12] Unlike his predecessor, Shoygu resumed the practice of addressing the general assembly of the Academy of Military Science, a key event in the Russian military calendar for summing up the results of the previous year.[13]

This balance between actual change and "polishing" suggests strongly that the direction of the Russian military is, at least for the time being, stable. Lieutenant-General Andrey Tretyak, former head of the General Staff's Main Operations Directorate, speaking in November 2012, said that the Russian government's current efforts are intended to "smooth the consequences" of previous reorganizations, and correct mistakes that resulted from following the "intuitive views and opinions of individual leaders, which did not always give the best result." Overall, he added, Shoygu and Gerasimov have an easier task than their predecessors, as the task ahead of them is much clearer.[14]

Thus, while there has been change at the top, the dominant characteristic of the transformation process now is continuity. Those expecting radical changes of direction with the appointment of Shoygu have been disappointed, and the eventual shape of the Russian military at the end of the transformation process is now finally becoming clear. As summarized by Fredrik Westerlund of Sweden's Defence Research Agency (FOI), "These were neither Serdyukov nor Shoygu reforms. They were Vladimir Putin reforms, with Ivanov, Serdyukov and Shoygu periods."[15]

2011 – THE NEW PHASE

This stable transition contrasts markedly with previous upheavals. The final destination, and indeed the direction of travel, of military transformation in Russia had long been unclear, with official announcements only serving to cloud the picture as they were countermanded, contradicted, rescinded, unachieved or in some cases simply ignored.[16] In this fluid context, it was dangerous to take for granted the next steps in Russia's modernization of its military. At the time of writing, the transformation effort has been under way for 5 years, and during most of this time, servicemen in Russia were expressing increasing disorientation and discontent at the relentless pace of change.

From 2008 to 2010, some of the fundamental aims of transformation were compromised by planning failures. For example, manpower planning relied on use of professional servicemen, but the retreat from wide-scale introduction of these "contractors" resulted in excessive churn of conscripts in units and a consequent sharp fall in average training standards. Meanwhile, implementation of procurement plans continued to show basic flaws in financial planning and reporting, which still pose a serious threat to transformation aims.

From early-2011, however, it appeared that transformation had entered a new and more stable phase, with more clearly articulated and realistic goals. It is the continuation of this process in 2012-13 that suggests that conclusions can now be drawn about the change program in Russia's armed forces and what those forces will look like at the end of this program.

Key personnel decisions taken before and after the 2012 Russian presidential elections already suggested that the transformation process was to continue on its current course with full support from President Putin. One of these indicators was the remarkable durability of Serdyukov in the face of perennial predictions of his imminent departure.[17] Serdyukov was one of the small minority of cabinet ministers to retain their posts in the major reshuffle following the presidential elections.

Furthermore, during the equally sweeping replacement of a large number of Russia's most senior military commanders in April and May 2012,[18] enthusiasts for reform were promoted to important roles, while those who questioned the process or objected to changes to their commands were retired or sidelined. This retention of the key actors who implemented the most radical reform seen in the Russian military for decades suggested that the process overall continued to enjoy President Putin's approval and support, and consequently that this reform was set to continue along its current path.

Backing Serdyukov.

The first stages of the fundamental overhaul of Russia's military implemented following the summer of 2008 have been well-documented in both Russian and foreign analyses.[19] A striking feature of the early stages of implementation of reform was strident and vociferous opposition to change from a broad sector of serving and retired military officers and defense officials. The reforms struck at some of the most deeply-held convictions about the nature of Russian military power, for example by moving away from the principle of mass mobilization, and in the process causing large numbers of mid-ranking officers who manned mobilization units to lose their jobs. A combination of direct career vulnerability and indirect concern for the future of Russia's defense capability led to trenchant opposition to initiatives by Serdyukov and his ally (CGS) Nikolai Makarov. A symptom and by-product of this opposition was innumerable hints, suggestions, and rumors that Serdyukov was to be fired for going too far in his efforts to overhaul the military — or in the view of his detractors, destroying it. It was therefore a mild surprise even to some of Serdyukov's backers that he was one of only five ministers to retain his post in the first government of Putin's latest presidency.

According to reporting by *Kommersant* newspaper, Serdyukov had come his closest to being retired in December 2011 when, at then-Prime Minister Putin's behest, Director of the Federal Security Service (FSB) Aleksandr Bortnikov had reviewed a list of potential replacements, including Deputy Prime Minister Dmitriy Rogozin. Rogozin was, supposedly, the only willing candidate, but Putin at that point decided to retain Serdyukov in order to see his reform process through to its conclusion.[20] The desire to avoid changing leadership in the midst of reform has been contrasted with a similar situation in the Ministry of Internal Affairs (MVD), which underwent its own traumatic upheaval but did not retain its chief, Rashid Nurgaliyev, in the same reshuffle. In theory, the MVD's reform process has been completed, thereby removing the need to retain Nurgaliyev despite his being a key Putin associate.

Nevertheless, reporting of Serdyukov's imminent sacking reached a crescendo of conviction shortly before the March 2012 presidential elections. Unattributed reports in some mass media criticized Serdyukov's ability to push through reform, and suggested that Rogozin could ease the friction between the Defence Ministry and industry, and thus successfully rearm the military. Notably, some of these reports cited "sources in the military-industrial complex" — in other words, people working under Rogozin's direction.[21]

Serdyukov, however, remained in place after the election. Once again, the fact that Serdyukov's reforms were incomplete was cited by observers as a main reason to retain him — along with his demonstrated loyalty to Putin and his willingness to take unpopular decisions. As noted by defense commentator Aleksandr Konovalov, "Serdyukov always goes for decisive steps with which the military are most often dissatisfied but which are requested from him by the bosses. None of the professional military would have acted this way."[22] Other suggested rationales for retaining Serdyukov instead of installing Rogozin included a desire not to give Rogozin too much political power and thereby risk creating a political rival to Putin himself.[23]

This reappointment of Serdyukov by newly-reinstated President Putin contrasted with repeated reports of friction between Serdyukov and Dmitriy Medvedev while Medvedev occupied the position of President (and Commander-in-Chief).[24] The perception that direction of the military sat more comfortably with Putin persisted throughout Medvedev's tenure. One characteristic report, albeit from a consistently outspoken and critical Russian commentator, claimed that "no-one is taking Medvedev seriously—he seems to have the authority to yell angrily at Serdyukov and other top ministers, but cannot make them do his bidding."[25] Yet even President Putin, at the first meeting of his latest term with senior military figures, appeared challenged by the problem of gripping the perennial issues of pay, manning, procurement, and housing—in effect, not far removed from the problems with the military that exercised Putin at the beginning of his first presidential term 12 years previously.[26]

This contrast in the relative relationships of the two presidents with the military under their command was brought into sharp relief shortly before the fourth anniversary of the armed conflict between Russia and Georgia, with the release online of a documentary video in which senior officers, including former CGS Yuriy Baluyevskiy, accused Medvedev of dithering and indecision in responding to the crisis in South Ossetia, Baluyevskiy in particular said that a decision to respond by Medvedev as commander-in-chief required "a kick up the arse" from Putin in Beijing, China.[27]

Although interpretations by commentators of the motivations behind the video were many and varied, there is general agreement that "there are plenty of 'offended generals' in the Russian army now, and directing their 'propaganda attack' against the current premier is not a difficult matter."[28] At the same time, the video gave fresh life both in Russia and abroad to the apparently moribund theory of competition, confrontation or at the very least, differences, between Putin and Medvedev.[29] But the forthright comment by Baluyevskiy is interesting, in particular because of his role as a key opponent of the principles of the current transformation process: Baluyevskiy was a principal actor in the production of Russia's most recent *Military Doctrine*, which was drafted during his tenure as CGS and released after he had been "retired" to the Security Council. This *Doctrine* therefore describes a military system that for Russia has already passed into history, with the armed forces already unrecognizable from their pre-2008 incarnation.[30]

As well as the Defence Minister, personnel changes within the military itself in May-June 2012 indicated strong support for continuing the current reform program.[31] Colonel-General Aleksandr Postnikov (also known as Postnikov-Streltsov) was appointed deputy CGS and at the time widely tipped as a successor to his patron, Makarov, in the top job.[32] Analysis as early as February 2006 had identified Postnikov as a key individual benefiting from the "stovepipe" promotion of Makarov and a number of reform-minded senior officers.[33] This appointment suggested that, despite losses along the way, there was still a cadre of Makarov protégés from Siberian Military District supporting his ideas on reform and in position to implement them.[34]

At the same time, reputed opponents of reform, including former Air Force Commander-in-Chief Colonel-General Aleksandr Zelin, were sidelined or dismissed—Zelin, allegedly, for opposing the method by which Russia's new Aerospace Defence Command was created[35] and for bypassing the chain of command to protest over educational reform for the air force.[36] The sacking of Zelin has also been attributed to his opposition to the way the new Aerospace Defence Command (VKO) was created.[37] Furthermore, shortly before his dismissal, Colonel-General Zelin had given an impressively long and detailed interview on the problems facing the reorganization of his command—indeed, the tone of the interview may not have inclined Serdyukov or other civilian leaders to retain him in place.[38] Zelin in particular highlighted command and control issues, and Russian commentators back him in questioning the effectiveness of subordinating air units to the OSK, arguing that this may lead to the "regionalization" of air power rather than its concentration.

This cull of the topmost ranks of the military left a cadre of supportive commanders occupying senior posts but at lower ranks than their predecessors. A subsequent round of promotions in early August 2012 appeared to confirm the new team in place by bringing newly-appointed senior commanders like Chief of the Navy Viktor Chirkov and VKO Oleg Ostapenko up to a rank commensurate with their status.[39] Personnel changes at the highest level since that date have not translated into reversals of reform decisions, and in particular, the removal of Serdyukov over issues unrelated to the main thrust of transformation have not indicated that President Putin disapproves of his achievements. As noted by eminent analyst of Russian defense economics Professor Julian Cooper, "Putin never criticised Serdyukov."[40]

STRATEGIC CONSIDERATIONS –
WHAT IS TRANSFORMATION FOR?

The overall direction of reform of Russia's military seems, therefore, to have been endorsed with approval at the highest level and so can be expected to continue unchanged. Curiously, however, some aspects of the assumptions driving this transformation remain unclear. In the early stages of reform, Serdyukov and Makarov were criticized for embarking upon major change without having first put in place the academic or theoretical basis for managing this change or defining the desired end state – a significant departure from previous Soviet and Russian practice.[41]

In the absence of a coherent narrative on the precise purpose of Russia's military – or perhaps in the presence of too many conflicting narratives – and with the shape of the military in direct contradiction to the current version of the *Military Doctrine*, which should define it, criticisms of this kind were echoed by more pessimistically inclined observers such as veteran commentator Pavel Felgenhauer:

> Serdyukov's military reform has been radical, but it lacked a clear strategic objective or a defined doctrine. The United States and NATO continued to be the presumed main enemy; and the Defense Ministry made massive investments into new strategic nuclear weapons and air defences. At the same time, attempts to meet all other possible threats resulted in thinly spreading out limited resources. Major military reform decisions have never been openly discussed in parliament or in the expert community.[42]

Even objective chroniclers of the Russian military noted with disquiet that the military was taking its final shape while the threats it is intended to counter were, in fact, still being defined.[43]

A particular symptom of lack of clarity over the military's purpose was the shifting role of the Russian navy. The fluctuating fortunes of the navy as a whole could be traced in the declared plans for building of capital ships. At the time of writing, aircraft carriers are once again promised for the medium term. But doubts remain over Russia's shipbuilding capability — accentuated by a succession of disappointments with the long-term submarine building and refit program, exemplified by delays and faults with the Severodvinsk and Aleksandr Nevsky.[44] Meanwhile, the repeated changes of direction in the debate over new capital ships left the Navy in a state of uncertainty. Often defined principally by financial arguments, these debates also hint at questions over the role and usage of a blue-water navy if there is no evident role for long-range power projection in the current military doctrine — the old adage being that the Russian military intervenes in places to which it can drive. The subordination of Russia's fleets to joint strategic commands gave rise to deep concern over what this entailed for prosecution of an independent maritime doctrine, and whether in effect it cemented the navy into the role of a supporting actor for land operations rather than an independent arm of service with its own doctrine[45] — in fact, according to Dmitry Gorenburg, the navy "has already largely been consigned to the role of a coastal protection force for the foreseeable future."[46] But the new role of the navy, even if defined in the minds of the reformers, does not appear to have been articulated publicly in doctrinal statements, giving rise to continuing uncertainty over the strategic purpose of Russian maritime power.

It appeared from the earliest stages of post-2008 change in the Russian armed forces that it was now clear to Serdyukov, Makarov and their supporters what the military was **not** needed for: namely, countering a massive land incursion by means of mobilized mass. While the idea of vulnerability to U.S. and North Atlantic Treaty Organization (NATO) hostile intentions remains strong, this vulnerability is finally no longer seen in Cold War-era conventional military terms. Instead, missile defense and information security in the broad Russian sense have come to the fore, even while lingering suspicions over a limited Libya-style intervention still provide a driving force for military modernization.[47]

At the same time, there remains a deep-seated failure to grasp that aggression against Russia in one form or another is not a key aim of NATO or U.S. policy—which stems from the even deeper failure to perceive that, in the current decade, it is no longer axiomatic that no significant problem can be addressed without Russian involvement. It is taken as read in Moscow that Russia matters, and the notion that Russia can be ignored is in itself felt as threatening.

This mindset of Russia's leadership and institutions compounds the problem of Russia misreading the assumptions and intentions of NATO and the United States. As noted by leading British commentator James Sherr:

> Russia ascribes intentions to its 'partners' that they do not hold. Neither in Kosovo, nor Iraq, nor Libya was Western policy 'about' Russia... The result is a misdiagnosis of threat and 'danger', a misallocation of resources and an 'aggravation of contradictions' on Rus-

sia's periphery that, by now, might have been settled. The connection, axiomatic to Moscow and unfathomable to Brussels, between NATO policy in the Balkans and the Caucasus primed the fuse for armed conflict in 2008, and one must hope (but dare not assume) that other spurious connections will not do so in future.

Further:

> The factors that frequently offset one another in a judicious threat assessment—capability, interest and intention—are invariably compounded in Russian threat assessments on the basis of worst-case assumptions. [48]

What is the Purpose of the Russian Military?

According to liberal Russian analyst Alexei Arbatov, "Contrary to the widespread belief among the Russian military-political elite, all objective parameters indicate that the threat of a major war is now (and in the future) less than ever in modern history."[49] In a joint publication with Vladimir Dvorkin, he continues the argument by suggesting that military preparations take no account of the state of relations with competitors, including the United States:

> Russian military policy has to a large extent existed in a way independently of the state's international direction... These contradictions. . . . suggest insufficient control by the political leadership over the military in developing the military doctrine as an important part of defence policy.[50]

Arbatov and Dvorkin go on to question Vladimir Putin's emphasis on military strength as the most important attribute of a great power:

We should not forget that the Soviet Union also relied entirely on military might and nuclear deterrence, but ended in disaster as a result of economic collapse and political paralysis. The USSR [Union of Soviet Socialist Republics] lost a global empire, sovereignty and territorial integrity, despite the fact that it had five or six times as many nuclear weapons as Russia, and a much smaller military-technical quality gap with the United States.[51]

Another leading Russian commentator, Sergey Karaganov, goes further in explaining Russia's perceived need for strong military forces: "It looks like the military buildup is expected to compensate for the relative weakness in other respects — economic, technological, ideological and psychological."[52]

Andrey Tretyak, while still a serving officer, explained that, while the:

likelihood of war is infinitesimal (*nichtozhnyy*), the Armed Forces exist against that likelihood. There is no specific enemy, and a very small likelihood of major war, but even though it is small it needs to be prepared for, wherever the attack may come from, whether a more or less technologically advanced enemy.[53]

This leaves the question of where this enemy can be found. According to FOI:

Up to 2020, the primary area of operations for the Army will probably remain Russia and its immediate surroundings. The Army's capability for operations outside Russia's territory is not necessarily dependent on the exact number of brigades and their location in each military district, but rather on whether they can, if required, be moved relatively quickly (within weeks or months).[54]

The fact that speed of movement is best achieved by different means in different parts of Russia was a key consideration in plans to introduce "light, medium, and heavy" brigades in Russia's ground forces, with procurement of wheeled armor[55] intended to provide for more agile, wheeled "light" units more suitable for intervention in Russia's Western neighbors with a well-developed road net.[56]

Further comments by Andrey Tretyak support the FOI assessment: In his words, there are no Russian plans for operations outside Russia except as part of an alliance, for example the Collective Security Treaty Organization (CSTO), or through bilateral agreements, for example with Armenia or Belarus. Therefore there are no plans, "not even the consideration of the possibility," of a military intervention in countries with no direct border with Russia.[57]

It has to be noted that a large number of countries do still have a direct border with Russia, and some of them will not be comforted by this. According to British academic and former soldier Rod Thornton, Russian foreign policy ambitions will "inevitably result in occasional Russian military interventions abroad."[58] The implement of choice for this, Thornton says, would be the Airborne Assault Forces (VDV) — still the most professional force available to Russia, and able to move with little visible preparation. Tretyak notes that "the VDV are not called rapid reaction forces, but fill that role."[59]

Thus it has to be recalled that use of military force has to be considered a useful foreign policy tool available to Russia, a concept validated by the outcome of the armed conflict in Georgia in August 2008, which, despite Western perceptions, resolved a number of key doctrinal challenges for Russia. As Arbatov and Dvorkin note, ahead of the conflict:

> All the warnings were not taken seriously, either by the U.S. or in NATO capitals—it was only the use of force that made an impression, which was openly admitted in the West. Moscow has also learned this lesson.[60]

RUSSIA'S HIERARCHY OF THREATS

According to prominent scholar of the Russian military, Stephen J. Cimbala:

> Russian military reform is endangered by continuing threat perceptions that exaggerate Russian military weakness and by domestic forces that play against a rational assessment of Russia's geostrategic requirements.[61]

A repeated criticism of Russia's current officially stated threat assessment is that it overstates the likelihood of armed attack from the United States and its allies, and that as a result, spending priorities and the transformation process overall are skewed and fail to address more realistic security threats to Russia. Arbatov and Dvorkin write that:

> It seems that once again, as is not rare throughout history, Russia is unprepared either militarily or politically for the real threat [and instead is] prioritising preparations for war with NATO on land, at sea and in air and space.[62]

There is a persistent argument, voiced by senior military commentators wielding prodigious authority in Russia, that foreign powers are planning to seize

Russia's natural resources, including by means of a paralyzing first strike by precision munitions against which Russia's air and space defenses will be entirely insufficient.[63] This provides the backdrop for repeated statements by Putin emphasizing defense against this eventuality. For instance, speaking at a meeting on implementing the 2011–20 state arms procurement program focusing on development of the technology base for air and space defence:

> We see that work is active around the world on developing high-precision conventional weapons systems that in their strike capabilities come close to strategic nuclear weapons. Countries that have such weapons substantially increase their offensive capability... Furthermore, there has been increasing talk among military analysts about the theoretical possibility of a first disarming, disabling strike, even against nuclear powers. This is something that we also need to take into account in our plans for developing the armed forces.[64]

Meanwhile, independent commentators like Sergey Karaganov dismiss these as as "phantasmagoric threats" which have "no bearing on reality and are nothing but caricature replicas of Soviet-era fantasies." This includes:

> Horror stories about the United States acquiring a capability for a massive attack on Russia with smart conventional missiles. Even if such missiles are ever created, the threat of a strike against Russian territory looks ridiculous as the retaliatory blow can be only a nuclear one.[65]

Nevertheless, it is this threat perception which is currently guiding Russia's funding priorities. According to Putin:

In accordance with the state arms procurement programme through to 2020, we will invest around 3.4
trillion roubles in developing our air and space de-
fences. This is around 20 percent—around 17 percent
to be more exact—of the total money earmarked for
re-equipping the armed forces.[66]

Spending on offensive weapons is also increased
as a direct result of this consideration. According to
the head of the General Staff's Center for Military-
Strategic Research (*Tsentr Voyenno-Strategicheskikh
Issledovaniy*—TsVSI), Sergey Chekinov, "Parity in offensive weapons with USA while USA develops BMD
is fundamental for strategic stability."[67] This reflects
the particular role that offensive nuclear weapons
play in the Russian defense psyche, as both a symbol
of great power status and a last-ditch guarantee of
sovereignty.[68] As put by Putin:

We will not under any circumstances turn our back
on the potential for strategic deterrence, and we will
reinforce it. It was precisely this which allowed us to
maintain state sovereignty during the most difficult
period of the 1990s.[69]

Stephen Cimbala adds essential perspective:

Russian military planners might reasonably assume
that the initial period of war can be one of great dan-
ger. What seems politically absurd in a day and age of
U.S.-Russian "reset" and post-post-Cold War Europe
is not necessarily impossible from the standpoint of
Russian military planners and analysts. Russian and
Soviet historical experience so dictates.[70]

Aerospace Defence Command.

The response to this perceived vulnerability to high-precision attack was the creation of VKO, notionally activated on December 1, 2011 but still in the process of development at the time of this writing.[71] The process of establishment of VKO has been subject to intense criticism, as for instance by Arbatov and Dvorkin:

> The formation of the Aerospace Defence Troops and the aerospace defence programme is not subject to clear military aims, does not have a logical command structure or a unified information system, and is not in accordance with the economic or military-technical capabilities of the country.[72]

But objections to its current structure miss the point that it is still in the process of integration into Russia's command and control system and is not scheduled to take on its full duties until 2015, with the integration continuing to 2020. On assuming the post of CGS, Gerasimov is said to have asked for "clarification" of the development of the VKO, but not to have suggested renouncing the changes made, since purchases of arms and equipment for the new command have been planned through 2020 and the only questions remaining are organizational ones.

According to Yuriy Aleksandrovich Levshov and other senior officers from the Russian General Staff Academy, the purpose of VKO is a response to the possibility of all campaigns being in air and space and not reaching the ground operations stage. It serves as a deterrent "so if an opponent is more technologically advanced, he must risk suffering unacceptable damage to prevent aggression." It is a "military response to a new threat for the medium and long term [according to] forecasts over decades — all possibilities. The task is not to allow the worst case scenario to develop."[73]

Other Threat Directions.

If any potential major adversary is mentioned in Russian discourse, it is almost inevitably one in the West. As always, the potential for a military threat from China is the exceptional case which, if discussed at all, is approached in exceedingly delicate terms. There is a mood of cautious optimism in assessments of relations with China.[74] The possibility of conflicts with countries that are not part of the Western bloc, including China, "is very unlikely to materialise because there are very few areas where Russian interests are at odds with the interests of these countries."[75] Furthermore:

> China, aware of its growing competition with the United States, including in the military-political sphere, is doing its utmost not to threaten Russia. True, there exists the problem of China's gaining too much strength, which in a situation where there is no energetic policy for development of the Trans-Baikal region may result in "Finlandization" of Russia, so to speak. But this risk is not a military one.[76]

Meanwhile, in the opinion of a range of authoritative commentators, the real security threat facing Russia is an entirely different one, from an entirely different direction — Russia's southern periphery. Arbatov and Dvorkin write that:

> A fundamental deficiency of military policy and the reform is that the system of priorities, emphasising

nuclear deterrence and aerospace defence (presuming confrontation and competition with the U.S. and its allies) does not address the real security threats, which arise from southern directions and are also connected with the proliferation of weapons of mass destruction and means of their delivery.[77]

Sergey Karaganov agrees, arguing that:

From the standpoint of military security [Russia] is in a situation that is unprecedented in its history. The country that for a thousand years has been building around the fundamental national idea—defense from outside threats and protection of its physical sovereignty—is no longer under threat and will have no risk of coming under threat in the medium term... Real threats of conflicts keep multiplying along Russia's southern borders. These conflicts will have to be prevented or neutralized in various ways, including the use of armed force. But these threats are fundamentally different from the existential ones that had shaped Russia's history for centuries.[78]

Ruslan Pukhov, of Moscow's authoritative Centre for Analysis of Strategies and Technologies (CAST) think tank, also agrees that the most likely military threat to Russia, ahead of the United States, is:

Post-Soviet type conflicts, both in Russia itself (in the form of separatist uprisings and attempts to secede) and similar conflicts with the neighbouring former Soviet republics. Most of these republics regard Russia as the main threat to their sovereignty, and are, therefore, interested in weakening Russian influence on their territory and internationally by all possible means.[79]

Cimbala, along with many Russian commentators, argues that it is this that should be the guiding influence for Russian defence planning:

> Russia is threatened neither primarily nor immediately by NATO. Instead, the threat of regional or smaller wars on Russia's periphery or terrorism and insurgent wars within Russia and other post-Soviet states must now take pride of place in General Staff and Ministry of Defense contingency planning. Preparedness for these contingencies of limited and local wars, regular and irregular, will require a smaller, more professional and more mobile military than post-Soviet Russia has fielded hitherto.[80]

Yet these preparations are not at present Russia's funding priority. According to Andrey Tretyak:

> The significance of ground forces is diminishing in modern war. The VDV are not called rapid reaction forces, but fill that role, so the VDV still have priority [for funding] over ground forces. What money the ground forces get goes to their funding priority, the Spetsnaz. So motor-rifle divisions are right at the back of the queue.[81]

The Southern Military District.

Despite apparent low priority in the funding queue and in presidential rhetoric, security issues affecting Russia from the south are not ignored. According to then Secretary of the Security Council Nikolai Patrushev, "Russia's steps are directed towards the construction, together with the former Union republics, of a system of security for the protection of our interests on the southern flank."[82] Despite capability improvements overall, including in the sensitive northwest of

Russia,[83] priority in re-equipment and reorganization is still going to the Southern Military District (MD). This continues a process started in South Ossetia,[84] where new units established after August 2008 were by October 2011 almost totally equipped with Russia's most up-to-date weapons systems.[85] A FOI study, when discussing the Southern MD, notes not only unusually high manning levels, and the greatest share of new arms and equipment, but also that the "Southern MD lacks equipment stores, which indicates an intention to be able to start fighting quickly with available assets."[86]

The emphasis on reorganization and re-equipment in the Southern MD indicates clearly enough that this is the area where Russia considers it most likely that the ground forces are likely to be employed in the foreseeable future. This arises not only from security concerns within Russia, but also over the next Western intervention, be it in Syria, Iran, or another candidate yet to emerge—reinforced by the persistent Russian perception, leaning on the examples of Afghanistan, Iraq, and Libya, that the United States and its allies do not always grasp the second- and third-order consequences of precipitate action. The private internal debate over for what precisely Russia **does** need a military is likely to have been influenced in later stages by the "mild panic" experienced by the Russian leadership when observing the fate of Muammar Gaddafi.[87]

To Euro-Atlantic eyes, the Middle East can appear tolerably remote from Russia; but this is to ignore Moscow's perception that "the approaches to Russia's borders" extend to a very considerable depth. According to Sherr, the Russian state has historically "maintained a set of security 'needs' out of kilter and scale with those of most European powers," leading to the need to address these needs by "creating client states and widening defence perimeters."[88] These wide perimeters of security consciousness mean that the consequences of military action in Syria or Iran would be seen as a direct security problem for Russia. According to Arbatov and Dvorkin, "In the near and medium term, destabilisation of South and Central Asia, the Near and Middle East, the South and North Caucasus are the greatest real military threat to Russia."[89]

In Russian perceptions, the Middle East is "right next door" (*sovsem ryadom*),[90] and there are not only complex political networks between the Middle East and former Soviet states like Azerbaijan, but also major influences from Muslim ideology and political processes in the North Caucasus. It is implicit in Russian thinking that the Russian Federation is a multi-confessional state and needs to manage its relations with the Islamic world accordingly.

Furthermore, bolstering military capacity in the Southern MD allows freedom of action in bringing hard influence to bear on Georgia with none of the doubts and disasters that attended the August 2008 intervention. According to one U.S. analyst:

> It is . . . quite clear that once the reforms are fully enacted, Russia's ability to project power outside its borders in regions other than the 'south' will be severely constrained.

But at the same time, the reforms will allow "increased capacity to perform successful military operations along [Russia's] southern periphery, which includes several former union republics of the USSR."[91]

Threat Responses — Nuclear.

When reviewing the nature of threats as perceived from Moscow and the means of countering them, one area needing special consideration is Russian activity in developing and introducing new types of strategic weapons while continuing strengths in nonstrategic nuclear weapons. The entry into force of the New Strategic Arms Reduction Treaty (START) treaty in February 2011 saw the start of intensive Russian activity aimed at developing and introducing new strategic weapons systems, including at least three new intercontinental ballistic missile (ICBM) programs. Tellingly, several of these are being conducted in conditions of secrecy, running counter to the common Russian habit of loudly proclaiming new advances in weapons technology.[92]

Nonstrategic nuclear weapons (NSNW) remain in the Russian inventory in large numbers and intended for use in a wide range of scenarios, including for "deescalation." Lying outside the bounds of New START, NSNW are, according to two Western analysts:

> prized and important assets to Moscow, and they have become even more prized and important assets as Russia's conventional military has become weaker. They are seen more and more as the fallback option if Russia one day faces some sort of defeat in a conventional conflict.[93]

"The result is that when a threat escalates from armed conflict to local war, we will have to go over to the use of nuclear weapons," agrees one leading Russian analyst.[94]

Thus while conventional forces remain in a state of transition, with a perceived decrease in their effectiveness, nuclear forces fill the deterrence gap in a manner reminiscent of the Russian armed forces' nadir in the late 1990s. Scenarios for the use of NSNWs can be deduced from exercises which culminate in their use: dangerously, however, NSNWs are not covered by public Russian doctrine, with, in addition, no transparency for effective deterrence.

This, plus current Russian efforts to develop precision very low yield and low collateral damage nuclear weapons, lends a keener edge to Russian statements on the possibility of pre-emptive strikes to neutralize perceived threats. At the time of this writing, the highest-profile example of this is a comment by CGS Makarov at the Moscow conference on Ballistic Missile Defence (BMD) on May 3-4, 2012—so often misleadingly or incompletely quoted that it is worth reproducing in full:

> Bearing in mind the destabilising nature of the missile defence system, specifically the creation of the illusion of carrying out a destructive strike with impunity, a decision on pre-emptive use of destructive means at our disposal will be taken during the period when the situation deteriorates. Deploying new strike weapons in the south and north-west of Russia for destroying the missile defence systems by fire, including the deployment of the Iskander missile complex in Kaliningrad Oblast, presents one of the possible options for destroying missile defence infrastructure in Europe.[95]

Despite the repetitiveness with which it is threatened, Iskander is far from the only means at Russia's disposal for the destruction of U.S. and allied BMD sites in Europe. Besides the NSNWs discussed above, developments in cruise missiles are seen by some analysts as alarming.[96] The deployment of S-400 missile systems to Kaliningrad presents particular interest, given their reported additional ground attack role.[97] Again, in contrast to the habitual noise and bluster surrounding threats of deploying Iskanders to Kaliningrad, this system has been deployed with no visible public announcement. This, together with the departure from the classic pattern of deploying Russia's most advanced anti-air and anti-missile capabilities around the capital first, argues that this deployment is a statement of intent that should be taken at least as seriously as the eventual Iskander move.

Regardless of the widespread attention it received, Makarov's statement on countering the BMD problem, in effect, contained nothing new; but it served as a useful reminder to those who consider that assurances of good intent will be sufficient to assuage Russian suspicion of BMD and the willingness to act on that suspicion. The continuing impasse over missile defense and promised Russian countermeasures have the potential to increase military tension in Central Europe to levels not seen since the end of the Cold War; as one analysis puts it, "hair triggers and tactical nuclear weapons are not comfortable bedfellows."[98] Meanwhile, according to President Putin speaking in July 2012, a key aim of the state arms program is not to compete in an arms race, but to ensure the "reliability and effectiveness of [Russia's] nuclear potential."[99]

PROCUREMENT AND REARMAMENT

In 2011, this arms purchasing program began and was scheduled to run to 2020. It attracted excited headlines and broke all records for the proposed level of spending.[100] The hugely ambitious rearmament plans, as well as the state of Russian armaments in service before it began, generated a wealth of statistics, but as always a dearth of meaningful and measurable ones — as noted earlier, a favorite index, the "percentage of modern weapons" available in service, is cited almost universally but never defined. What hard figures do exist, particularly on the number of weapons systems actually arriving in service, are generally discouraging. Leading commentator on the transformation process Dmitry Gorenburg has singled out the example of the Pantsir-S air defense system as "a good example of how, for all the worry about a massive Russian rearmament program, this rearming has been pretty slow thus far."[101]

Slow deliveries need to be seen against the backdrop of on-going infighting between the defense industry and the Ministry of Defence and General Staff. This public spat reached a peak ahead of the March 2012 presidential elections,[102] with President Putin backing the defense industry against those who argued that its output was no longer fit for its purpose. One of the key tasks of Deputy Prime Minister Dmitriy Rogozin, in his new role as defense and space industry supremo, was to bring order to the procurement process. This involved heavy criticism of the defense industry — while never quite in direct opposition to Putin — and the willingness to trample vested interests, as witness his role advocating the cancellation of flagship procurement projects such as the BMP-3 and BMD-4M.[103]

But the changes that Rogozin apparently wished to introduce were so deep, and the challenges to ingrained assumptions so severe, that progress was slow and painful, and reverses are common. There were continuing instances of open discord between Rogozin and Nikolai Makarov,[104] including over plans to produce a next-generation strategic bomber.[105] Meanwhile, Rogozin's personal style, not diminished in the slightest on his return to Russia from his colorful tenure as head of the Russian Mission to NATO, kept colleagues, opponents, and observers equally alert—not least through his continuing habit of causing havoc with unexpected announcements released via Twitter and shortly afterwards issuing retractions or explanations.[106] Rogozin sought to introduce a number of measures intended to impose or enforce control, including the creation of a "Council for State-Private Partnership," intended to "combat monopolism in the military-industrial complex."[107]

Nonetheless, pragmatic decisions on equipment purchasing and disposal are now being made that appear more closely related to Russia's force optimization goals and purchasing capability, for example, the purchase of Su-30SM multirole aircraft—a localized variant of the Su-30MKI as successfully supplied to India. This is an aircraft that should, in theory and despite noises to the contrary by the manufacturers, be well within Russian capabilities to produce early and in significant quantities.[108] At the other end of the service lifespan, the long-awaited trimming of the tank fleet appears to have started in earnest, with disposal of T-64, T-55, and even T-80 models finally under way.[109] Thus at least in some areas, equipment programs are beginning to fall in line with plans for reorganized and better equipped units in the individual commands.

At the same time, the over-ambitious nature of the procurement plans was noted immediately on their announcement and is now becoming clear.[110] Both the capabilities of the defense industry,[111] and the funding allocated, were questioned. As put by Aleksei Arbatov, "Russia declares clearly unrealistic plans for the armed forces' re-equipment, whose failure will once again damage the country's prestige."[112]

A denial of reality long colored the debate over funding for procurement,[113] even well after former Minister of Finance Aleksey Kudrin was induced to resign after he pointed out that the plans were unaffordable.[114] On his pre-election tours, Putin would point out that, after the current spending plans, "there is no more money" — but not that there was not enough even to cover those plans.[115] Later, in June 2012, Putin re-emphasized that defense orders must be filled as agreed by manufacturers, and no further funds would be forthcoming:

> There won't be other money, greater than the amount allocated to 2020. I've already talked about this 100 times. At one recent conference, proposals were again heard to increase it. We would be happy to increase it, perhaps, but there's no money![116]

Financial constraints were exacerbated by ongoing difficulties in administering procurement and restarting production in moribund facilities — problems that caused parts of the State Defence Order to be postponed for 3 years at an early stage of implementation.[117] Most recently at the time of this writing, the Ministry of Finance has issued a weighty report on budget spending that is harshly critical of the arms procurement program and will make uncomfortable reading for anyone involved in defense spending.[118]

CONTINUING CHALLENGES TO REFORM

Difficulties in pushing through ambitious procurement plans are not the only obstacle to realizing the desired new shape of the Russian military. The hangover from the long period of stagnation in military spending and development also has direct effects in individual arms of service. One indicative symptom is the air force continuing to suffer from a failure to retain junior officers, despite huge increases in salaries. Flying hours were only being allocated to senior officers — a problem that was supposed to have been rectified at the early stages of increased funding, with fuel provision for the air force as part of the general increase in military spending realized from Russia's increased oil revenues from 2005 onwards.[119] The fact that fundamental issues such as this have not been resolved by the simple provision of money is indicative of the extent to which Russia's military was degraded during the years of relative neglect prior to 2005.

Many of Russia's remaining problems in implementing its transformation aims are to do, not with money or equipment, but with people. As noted by Arbatov and Dvorkin:

> The traditional Russian and Soviet approach has always been, from the times of the regular army and the wars of Peter the Great, down to the Second Chechen Campaign in 1999-2000, that servicemen are the Army and the Navy's cheapest 'consumable'.[120]

Now, under fundamentally new circumstances where demographic change means that servicemen are at a premium, and furthermore that they each require greater investment in order to be trained in operating ever more sophisticated equipment, this approach needs fundamental revision. But difficulties in implementing plans for professional noncommissioned officers (NCOs), and for managing manpower overall, show that progress is slow.

NCOs.

The selection and training of NCOs is a particularly difficult challenge, for Russia's transformation aims. Despite early recognition of the importance of developing NCOs into more effective leaders, administrators, and operators, very little progress appears to have been made. Reporting in early-2012 suggested that some NCOs were still undergoing the 10-month warrant officer (*praporshchik*) course in order to fill administrative posts — despite the fact that *praporshchiki* had notionally been abolished. Meanwhile, poor planning and basic failures of arithmetic in predicting the required numbers of officer cadets led to several thousands of cadets graduating from military academies as officers, but continuing to serve as NCOs.[121]

June 2012 saw the graduation of the first "long-course" NCO cadets from the Ryazan Airborne Forces Institute. The course, lasting over 2 years, saw 241 enrolled, with 180 graduating the course.[122] In November 2012, 175 cadets graduated out of 240 accepted,[123] and another 124 NCOs are expected to graduate in 2013. The tiny numbers of graduates, and the length of the course, bring the extent of the challenge into perspective when compared with the requirement for tens of thousands of trained and effective NCOs in order to meet Russia's ambitions for its military. This pace makes a mockery of the declared target for numbers of professionally trained NCOs. One result is the announcement by Shoygu in February 2013 that some 55,000 warrant officer posts were to be reintroduced. At the time of this writing, it remains unclear whether this is intended as an interim fix or a permanent solution.

Lieutenant-General Andrey Tretyak explains the small numbers graduating from Ryazan by stating that the NCO courses of 2.5-3 years are still experimental. Russia has never had NCOs in the sense understood in other armies, he notes, and foreign experience in creating an NCO cadre was examined but rejected as not appropriate for Russia—so Russia developed its "own national program."

Tretyak went on to explain a fundamental difference between Russian and Western practice in selection of individuals with the right leadership skills for NCO training. In Russia, leadership is tested during the 2-3 year training course—not assessed before selection for training. If leadership skills are not detected during this period, then the candidate goes on to a technical post instead of a leadership position. The challenge of junior leadership, he concludes, remains a new and difficult one for the Russian military.[124]

The problem was formally recognized in May 2012, with the announcement that over 10,000 posts, downgraded to be filled by NCOs, would revert to requiring commissioned officers.[125] This followed sustained reporting of units being unable to carry out their functions since the NCOs or conscripts tasked with carrying out duties previously assigned to officers simply did not have the training or experience to do so, with examples including an anti-air missile unit deciding on its own initiative to rehire dismissed officers after exercises proved conscripts were incapable of commanding Buk systems.[126] In the move to "professional" NCOs, as with the development of officer manning overall, the Russian military's ambitions have run ahead of what is possible without detailed long-term planning and a corresponding fundamental cultural shift in the understanding of what precisely effective noncommissioned servicemen are and how they are formed.

Manpower and Training.

It has been apparent to observers both within and outside the Russian Federation since well before the start of the current reforms that a reduction in the conscription term from 2 years to 1 would be the beginning of a slow-motion disaster for the Russian military's manpower plans.[127] Five years later, Russia is continuing to scramble to broaden the conscription pool and debates continue over deferments for students, accepting conscripts with a criminal record, and even extending conscription liability to the age of 30.[128] Meanwhile, the fiction is maintained at the highest level that Russia enjoys a "million-man army," despite the impossible nature of this claim being demonstrated again and again.[129] Privately, senior Russian officers recognize that the one million figure is unreal, even when taken to refer to posts not people, but argue that the difference between the target figure of one million and actual numbers is not as large as suggested in the media—the rolling deficit (*tekushchiy nekomplekt*) is partially filled from the reserve. They add that there is no aim to actually reach one million men under arms during peacetime.[130]

In the meantime, those men and women that do arrive in the military are faced with an accelerated training program whose nature depends on the time of year they are called up. Stephen Cimbala notes that:

> Many of the 'permanent readiness' brigades would be undermanned and not capable of combat deployment with their full complement of personnel. Further, most of the troops are conscripts serving 1-year terms and called up twice each year: at any given time, half of them have been in uniform less than 6 months and lack adequate training for battle.[131]

FOI agrees:

> Although the Armed Forces often send new recruits on exercises and even commit them to combat operations, shorter training time means that both individual soldiers, and consequently their units, have a reduced capability.[132]

There are clearly limitations on what 12-month conscripts are capable of. This is tacitly recognized in decisions like the 31st Detached Guards Air Assault Brigade being assigned an additional "peacekeeping" function "because it is [the unit] with the highest proportion of contract manning."[133]

Meanwhile, the ground forces retain a higher proportion of conscript manpower, while contract servicemen are more prominent in permanent readiness units and posts involving more challenging tasks, as for instance in the navy, VKO, or VDV. But the range of posts for which a 12-month conscript can be trained usefully continues to narrow. As Aleksei Arbatov points out:

> Plans to keep the number of conscripts, serving 12-month compulsory military service, at more than 30 percent of the armed forces' personnel are at vari-

ance with plans to introduce new sophisticated weapons systems and military equipment and methods of conducting intensive operations.[134]

On occasion, this gives rise to alarm over personnel performance in Russia's intensifying series of major exercises, as the proportion of servicemen with very little experience rises.[135] Major-General Aleksandr Rogovoy describes the current round of exercises as an assessment (*aprobatsiya*) of new forms and methods of utilization of troops and forces.[136] As such, they have highlighted deficiencies in training not just among conscripts, but also among officers, especially in those scenarios involving joint operations. A large number of officers are not used to working with other services and do not know their specific features.[137] Furthermore, according to anecdotal evidence, the Kavkaz 2012 exercise demonstrated that officers were losing the ability to work without information systems—so they ran into difficulties when their information support and command and control systems were switched off. It was determined that training for operations against an opponent with total information superiority required "teaching officers to work with paper maps again, not electronic ones."[138]

CONCLUSION AND POLICY IMPLICATIONS

The current transformation of the Russian armed forces marks the final demise of the Soviet military, with a decisive step away from the cadre unit and mass mobilization structure inherited from the USSR. This transformation is intended to meet threats as they are perceived from Moscow, not from any other capital. According to Putin, "The changing geopolitical situation requires rapid and considered action. Russia's armed forces must reach a fundamentally new capability level within the next 3-5 years."[139]

After the application of shock therapy to the military in the autumn of 2008 and subsequent twists and turns in both policy and implementation that left Russian officers joking about roller-coasters and about their new secret weapon being complete unpredictability, 2011 saw the beginning of a more smooth and stable transformation process. This qualitatively new phase affected all areas of military reform and—in all probability—has shaped the force that will emerge after the reform process is deemed complete.[140]

In part, this appeared to be due to new supervisory arrangements at the highest level, with the Security Council of the Russian Federation (SCRF) now approving reform plans.[141] The apparent effect was to introduce stability not only by planning further ahead than in the early stages of reform, but also by providing a more methodical approach—with fewer instances of the Minister of Defence attracting criticism for enthusiastically embracing ideas from abroad without first assessing their suitability for Russian conditions.[142] But this latest phase of reform has continued with little adjustment through a change of defense leadership with the arrival of Shoygu as Minister of Defence in November 2012.

It follows that the impact on the direction of reform of leadership change at anything less than a presidential level should not be overstated. At the same time, it is essential to pay continuing attention to the aims and goals of the transformation process, since they are directly relevant to the military security not only of Russia's immediate neighbors, but also of those states who Russia sees as a competitor, including the United States.

Deep and persistent challenges, including problems with manning, funding, and procurement, mean that many ambitions for the Russian military will not be achieved in the short- to medium-term. All the same, it is undoubtedly the case that post-transformation Russia will have a very different force available from the one which went into action in Georgia in 2008, and one that is more effective, flexible, adaptable, and scalable for achieving Russia's foreign policy aims.[143] The depth and scale of change which the Russian military has undergone in the last 5 years is impossible to overstate, and few of the certainties that underpinned analysis of Russian military capability in the last decade still hold good. The striking differences in equipment and uniforms that were apparent when watching parade rehearsals on Moscow's Tverskaya Street in April 2013 may be largely cosmetic, but the fact that Russian servicemen now resemble those of a modern military instead of their previous plainly post-Soviet appearance is also symbolic of much deeper transformation, and of readiness to change further. As noted by FOI, "Although Russia will probably not be able to reach all of the ambitious goals of its reform programme for the Armed Forces, there is little doubt that its overall military capability will have increased by 2020."[144]

The advice given to President Putin on what precisely is achievable using the military will be broader accordingly. Critically, it can be expected that the military's role as a tool in Russian foreign policy — validated for Russia by the medium-term outcomes of the armed conflict with Georgia — will still be at odds with what is considered normal behavior in international relations in 21st century Europe.[145]

ENDNOTES

1. Among many other examples, see "Russian Military Reform from Administrative Reorganization to Structural Reform," Presentation by Andrey Frolov and Mikhail Barabanov, Washington, DC, U.S. National Defense University, Center for Analysis of Strategies and Technologies (CAST), April 26, 2012.

2. Author interviews with Russian officers, who preferred to remain anonymous, in late-2012.

3. Keir Giles, "Where Have All the Soldiers Gone? Russia's Military Plans Versus Demographic Reality," Shrivenham, UK: Conflict Studies Research Centre, October 2006, available from *www.academia.edu/929850/Where_Have_All_the_Soldiers_Gone_ Russias_Military_Plans_Versus_Demographic_Reality/*.

4. Märta Carlsson, Johan Norberg, and Fredrik Westerlund, "Military Capability of Russia's Armed Forces in 2013," *Russian Military Capability in a Ten-Year Perspective—2013*, Stockholm, Sweden: FOI, forthcoming.

5. Viktor Litovkin, "*Prezident ne ostavil armii vybora—kurs na reformy budet prodolzhen*" ("The President Gives the Army No Choice: The Reform Path Will Continue"), *Nezavisimoye voyennoye obozreniye*, March 8, 2013, available from *nvo.ng.ru/nvo/2013-03-08/1_president.html*.

6. "Expanded Meeting of the Defence Ministry Board," Russian presidential website, February 27, 2013, available from *eng. Kremlin.ru/transcripts/5050*.

7. Vladimir Mukhin, "*Glavkoverkh beret Genshtab pod lichnyy control*" ("Supreme Commander Takes General Staff under Personal Control"), *Nezavisimoye voyennoye obozreniye*, December 17, 2012, available from *www.ng.ru/wars/2012-12-17/1_genshtab.html*.

8. Märta Carlsson, "The Structure of Power—An Insight into the Russian Ministry of Defence," Stockholm, Sweden: FOI, November 2012.

9. Dmitri Trenin, "Russia's New Tip of the Spear," *Foreign Policy*, Vol. 8, May 2013, available from *carnegie.ru/2013/05/08/russia-s-new-tip-of-spear/g2ti.*

10. "Russia's Defence Strategy Submitted to the President," Russian presidential website, January 29, 2013, available from *eng. news.Kremlin.ru/news/4906.*

11. Katri Pynnöniemi, "Russia's Defence Reform," Briefing Paper 126, Helsinki, Finland: Finnish Institute of International Affairs (FIIA), March 2013.

12. "*Vossozdany gvardeiskaia Tamanskaia ordena Oktiabrskoi Revoliutsii Krasnoznamennaya ordena Suvorova motostrelkovaia i Kantemirovskaia ordena Lenina Krasnoznamennaia tankovaia divizii*" ("Tamanskaya Guards Order of the October Revolution Red Banner Order of Suvorov Motor-Rifle and Kantemirovskaya Order of Lenin Red Banner Tank Divisions Restored"), Russian Ministry of Defence website, May 4, 2013, available from *stat.function.mil.ru/news_page/country/more.htm?id=11735703@egNews.*

13. Viktor Litovkin, "*Akademiki analiziruyut reformu*" ("Academicians Analyse the Reform"), *Nezavisimoye voyennoye obozreniye,* February 1, 2013, available from *nvo.ng.ru/realty/2013-02-01/1_reform.html.*

14. Speaking at a briefing at NATO Defense College, Rome, Italy, November 27, 2012.

15. Private comment, September 5, 2013.

16. For an overview of the many changes of plan and direction in the current round of Russian military transformation, see "Chronology of Military Reforms since 2008," in Marcel de Haas, *Russia's Military Reforms: Victory after Twenty Years of Failure?* Clingendael Papers No. 5, The Hague, The Netherlands: Netherlands Institute of International Relations, November 2011.

17. For a particularly vitriolic example, see Konstantin Sivkov, "*Serdyukov ne prosto nepopulyaren – on omerzitelen*" (Serdyukov is not just unpopular, he is repellent), *KM-Novosti,* May 17, 2012, available from *www.km.ru/v-rossii/2012/05/17/ministerstvo-oborony-rf/k-sivkov-serdyukov-ne-prosto-nepopulyaren-omerzitelen.*

18. Vladislav Kulikov, "*Medvedev proizvel kadrovyye peres-tanovki v voyskakh*" (Medvedev carried out personnel reshuffles in the forces), *Rossiyskaya Gazeta*, May 6, 2012, available from *www.rg.ru/2012/05/06/oficeri-site.html*.

19. Among many others, see Mikhail Barabanov, ed., *Novaya Armiya Rossii*, Moscow, Russia: *Tsentr analiza strategiy i tekhnologiy*, 2010; Bertil Nygren, Roger McDermott, and Carolina Pallin, eds., *The Russian Armed Forces in Transition*, New York: Routledge, 2012; Bettina Renz and Rod Thornton, "Russian Military Modernization. Cause, Course and Consequence," *Problems of Post-Communism*, Vol. 50, No. 1, January/February 2012.

20. Ivan Safronov, "*Minoborony vypalo v ostatok*," *Kommersant*, May 21, 2012, available from *www.kommersant.ru/doc/1939822*.

21. See for example Moskovskiy Komsomolets, March 13, 2012; Argumenty Nedeli, February 29, 2012.

22. Ekho Moskvy radio, May 21, 2012. See also commentators Leonid Razikhovskiy in *Rossiyskaya Gazeta*, Vadim Solovyev in *Kommersant-Vlast*, Viktor Ozerov on *RIA-Novosti*, all on May 21, 2012.

23. See for example *Profil*, March 26, 2012; and *Novaya Gazeta*, March 19, 2012.

24. Unlike the majority of ministers, Serdyukov is constitutionally answerable to the president, not to the prime minister.

25. Pavel Felgenhauer, "Solomonov Attacks Defense Ministry For Holding Back Funds," *Eurasia Daily Monitor*, Vol. 8, Issue 130, July 7, 2011. See also Pavel Felgenhauer, "The Failure of Military Reform in Russia," *Eurasia Daily Monitor*, Vol. 9, Issue 123, June 28, 2012.

26. "*Vstrecha s rukovodstvom Minoborony*," *Kremlin.ru*, May 30, 2012, available from *Kremlin.ru/transcripts/15508*.

27. "Lost Day: The Whole Truth About The War 08.08.08," available from *www.youtube.com/watch?v=sYQeeFXhOQw*.

28. Open Source Center (OSC), "Internet Film Accusing Medvedev of Delaying Military Action Against Georgia Eyed," *Politkom.ru*, August 13, 2012.

29. As, for example, in *"Rossiyskaya elita na grani raskola,"* Pik TV, August 9, 2012, discussing analysts' suggestions of "the beginning of a campaign against Dmitriy Medvedev and a symbol of a split in the tandem," available from *pik.tv/ru/news/story/44626-rossiyskaia-elita-na-grani-raskola*. See also Catherine Belton, "Rift Grows Between Putin and Medvedev," *Financial Times*, August 10, 2012.

30. Keir Giles, "The Military Doctrine of the Russian Federation 2010," Rome, Italy: NATO Defense College, February 2010, available from *www.conflictstudies.org.uk/files/MilitaryDoctrine_RF_2010.pdf*.

31. "Russian president appoints, dismisses several senior military commanders," Moscow, Russia: OSC, *Kremlin.ru*, April 27, 2012.

32. *"Naznachen novyy nachalnik Genshtaba,"* Argumenty Nedeli, May 4, 2012, available from *www.argumenti.ru/army/n338/174844*.

33. As cited in Giles: "Georgia: Lessons Learned."

34. Sergey Ishchenko, *"Generalskaya uborka,"* Svobodnaya pressa, April 27, 2012.

35. Ivan Gladilin, *"Voyennyy tandem pristupil k 'zachistke kadrov',"* KM-Novosti, April 28, 2012, available from *www.km.ru/v-rossii/2012/04/28/organy-vlasti-rf/voennyi-tandem-pristupil-k-zachistke-kadrov*.

36. *"Naznachen novyy nachalnik Genshtaba,"* Argumenty Nedeli, May 4, 2012, available from *www.argumenti.ru/army/n338/174844*.

37. At the time of this writing, the establishment of the new command and the precise extent of its duties and how they overlapped with those of the air force appeared still controversial, with open sources contradictory, and Russian interviewees unwilling or unable to comment.

38. Viktor Litovkin, "*7 aviabaz, 28 modernizirovannykh aerodromov i noveyshiye samolety. Glavnokomanduyushchiy VVS Rossii general-polkovnik Aleksandr Zelin rasskazal 'NVO' o razvitii otechestvennoy voyennoy aviatsii*" (Seven airbases, 28 modernised aerodromes and the newest aircraft. Russian Air Force C-in-C Col-Gen Aleksandr Zelin tells NVO about the development of Russian military aviation), *Nezavisimoye voyennoye obozreniye*, March 16, 2012.

39. "*Ukaz o prisvoenii voinskikh zvaniy vysshikh ofitserov voyennosluzhashchim Vooruzhennykh Si*" (Order on awarding flag ranks to servicemen of the Armed Forces), *Kremlin.ru*, August 9, 2012, available from *news.Kremlin.ru/acts/16199*.

40. Private comment, September 5, 2013.

41. See, among others, Nygren, McDermott and Pallin, eds.

42. Felgenhauer.

43. Boris Sokolov, "*Orientirovat Vooruzhennye Sily nado na otrazheniye realnykh, a ne fantasticheskikh ugroz*" (We need to direct the Armed forces at repelling real threats, not fantasy ones), *Voyenno-promyshlennyy kuryer*, August 8, 2012, available from *vpk-news.ru/articles/9127*.

44. See Thomas Nilsen, "Brand new attack submarine not ready for service," *Barents Observer*, January 24, 2012, available from *barentsobserver.com/en/briefs/brand-new-attack-submarine-not-ready-service* and related reports at *barentsobserver.com/en/security/nuclear-submarine-needs-more-testing* and *barentsobserver.com/en/security/dozens-major-flaws-newest-submarine*.

45. See "The Role of the Navy" in Giles, "Russian Operations in Georgia."

46. Dmitry Gorenburg, "Predictions on Future Russian Air Force Procurement," Russian Military Reform blog, July 10, 2012, available from *russiamil.wordpress.com/2012/07/10/predictions-on-future-russian-air-force-procurement/*.

47. Keir Giles, "The State of the NATO-Russia Reset," Shrivenham, UK: Conflict Studies Research Centre, September 2011.

48. James Sherr, "Russia and the Rest of Us: The Dynamics of Discontent," Carlisle, PA: Strategic Studies Institute, U.S. Army War College, August 2012.

49. Alexei Arbatov, "Real and Imaginary Threats: Military Power in World Politics in the 21st Century," *Russia in Global Affairs*, April 15, 2013, available from *carnegie.ru/2013/04/15/real-and-imaginary-threats/g0ms#.*

50. Aleksey Arbatov and Vladimir Dvorkin, "*Voyennaya reforma Rossii: sostoyaniye i perspektivy*" ("Russia's Military Reform: Status and Prospects"), Moscow, Russia: Carnegie Centre, 2013, p. 16.

51. *Ibid.*, p. 23.

52. Sergey Karaganov, "Security Strategy: Why Arms?" *Russia in Global Affairs*, October 26, 2012, available from *eng.globalaffairs.ru/pubcol/Security-Strategy-Why-Arms-15716.*

53. Speaking at a briefing at NATO Defense College, Rome, Italy, November 27, 2012.

54. Carolina Vendil Pallin, ed., "Russian Military Capability in a Ten-Year Perspective—2011," FOI, August 2012, p. 124.

55. Aleksey Nikolskiy, "*Rossiya ispytyvayet italyanskiye kolesnyye tanki*" ("Russia testing Italian wheeled tanks"), *Vedomosti.ru*, May 12, 2012, available from *www.vedomosti.ru/politics/news/1732497/rossiya_ispytyvaet_italyanskie_tanki.*

56. Kristopher Rikken, "Meanwhile, Over at the Massive Russian Military Buildup. . .," ERR News, February 13, 2013, available from *news.err.ee/582a4ad5-d634-40b4-b3c7-b2f26e6071a3.*

57. Speaking at a briefing at Rome, Italy, NATO Defense College, November 27, 2012.

58. Rod Thornton, *Organizational Change in the Russian Airborne Forces: The Lessons of the Georgian Conflict*, Carlisle, PA: Strategic Studies Institute, U.S. Army War College, December 2011.

59. *Ibid.*

60. Arbatov and Dvorkin, p. 19.

61. Stephen J. Cimbala, "Russian Threat Perceptions and Security Policies: Soviet Shadows and Contemporary Challenges," *The Journal of Power Institutions in Post-Soviet Societies*, Issue 14/15, 2013, available from *pipss.revues.org/4000*.

62. Arbatov and Dvorkin, p. 29.

63. As, for instance, in Makhmut Gareyev, "*Na poroge epokhi potryaseniy: dlya obespecheniya bezopasnosti trebuyetsya obyektivnaya otsenka ugroz*" (On the threshold of an epoch of upheaval: in order to provide security, an objective assessment of the threats is required), *Voyenno-promyshlennyy kuryer*, No. 3, January 23, 2013, p. 471.

64. "Meeting on implementing the 2011–2020 state arms procurement programme," Russian presidential website, June 19, 2013, available from *eng.Kremlin.ru/transcripts/5615*.

65. Sergey Karaganov, "Security Strategy: Why Arms?" *Russia in Global Affairs*, October 26, 2012, available from *eng.globalaffairs.ru/pubcol/Security-Strategy-Why-Arms-15716*.

66. "Meeting on implementing the 2011–2020 state arms procurement programme."

67. Speaking at a briefing at NATO Defense College, Rome, Italy, November 27, 2012.

68. See also Keir Giles, "Ballistic Missile Defence and Russia," forthcoming publication.

69. Vladimir Putin, "*Byt silnymi: garantiya natsionalnoy bezopasnosti dlya Rossii*" ("Being strong is a guarantee of national security for Russia"), *Rossiyskaya gazeta*, February 20, 2012.

70. Stephen J. Cimbala, "Russian Threat Perceptions and Security Policies: Soviet Shadows and Contemporary Challenges," *The Journal of Power Institutions in Post-Soviet Societies*, Issue 14/15, 2013, available from *pipss.revues.org/4000*.

71. For a detailed analysis of the development of the VKO, see Colonel-General Viktor Yesin, *"Rossiyskiye vozdushno-kosmicheskiye voyska i programma vooruzheniya"* ("Russian Aerospace Troops and the Armaments Program"), in Arbatov and Dvorkin (eds.), *Protivoraketnaya oborona: protivostoyaniye ili sotrudnichestvo?* (Missile defence: confrontation or cooperation?), Moscow, Russia: Carnegie Centre, 2012, pp. 141-159.

72. Arbatov and Dvorkin, p. 71.

73. Speaking at a briefing at NATO Defense College, Rome, Italy, November 27, 2012.

74. Vasiliy Kashin, "The Sum Total of All Fears. The Chinese Threat Factor in Russian Politics," *Russia in Global Affairs*, April 15, 2013, available from *eng.globalaffairs.ru/number/The-Sum-Total-of-All-Fears-15935*.

75. Ruslan Pukhov, "The World vs Russia," *Force*, August 2013, available from *www.forceindia.net/TheWorldvsRussia.aspx*.

76. Sergey Karaganov, "Security Strategy: Why Arms?" *Russia in Global Affairs*, October 26, 2012, available from *eng.globalaffairs.ru/pubcol/Security-Strategy-Why-Arms-15716*.

77. Arbatov and Dvorkin, p. 5.

78. Karaganov.

79. Ruslan Pukhov, "The World vs Russia," *Force*, August 2013, available from *www.forceindia.net/TheWorldvsRussia.aspx*.

80. Cimbala.

81. Speaking at a briefing at NATO Defense College, Rome, Italy, November 27, 2012.

82. Interview with Security Council Secretary Nikolai Patrushev, "The real threats for Russia, the USA and the EU lie in the current instability," *Kommersant*, January 12, 2012.

83. Stefan Forss, Lauri Kiianlinna, Pertti Inkinen, and Heikki Hult, "Venäjän sotilaspoliittinen kehitys ja Suomi" (The Development of Russian Military Policy and Finland), Series 2: Research Reports No. 47, Helsinki, Finland: Finnish National Defence University, 2011.

84. Keir Giles, "Understanding the Georgian Conflict, Two Years On," Rome, Italy: NATO Defense College, September 2011, available from *www.ndc.nato.int/research/series.php?icode=9*.

85. Sergey Konovalov, "*Obnovlennaya oborona Severnogo Kavkaza. Generaly otchitalis o prakticheski polnom perevooruzhenii voysk v regione*" ("Renewed defence of the North Caucasus. Generals report on the almost complete rearmament of troops in the region"), *Nezavisomoye voyennoye obozreniye*, October 25, 2011, available from *www.ng.ru/nvo/2011-10-25/6_kavkaz.html*.

86. Carlsson, Norberg and Westerlund.

87. "*Zapreshchennoye nastupleniye: Intervyu prezidenta Akademii geopoliticheskikh problem general-polkovnika Leonida Ivashova*" ("Forbidden offensive: Interview with the President of the Academy of Geopolitical Problems, Col-Gen Leonid Ivashov"), *Segodnya*, March 8, 2012, available from *www.segodnia.ru/content/106674*.

88. Sherr.

89. Arbatov and Dvorkin, p. 29.

90. Andrey Tretyak, speaking at a briefing at NATO Defense College, Rome, Italy, November 27, 2012.

91. Gregory Lannon, "Russia's New Look Army Reforms and Russian Foreign Policy," *The Journal of Slavic Military Studies*, Vol. 24, No. 1, pp. 26-54, February 2011.

92. Mark B. Schneider, "Russian Nuclear Modernization," Presentation at National Institute for Public Policy, Fairfax, VA, June 20, 2012.

93. Renz and Thornton.

94. Konstantin Sivkov, as quoted in Lannon.

95. As cited in *Vzglyad* newspaper, available from *www.vz.ru/politics/2012/5/3/577140.html*. Transcripts and slides of presentations made by the United States at the same conference are available from *moscow.usembassy.gov/missile_defense.html*.

96. Dennis M. Gormley, "Cruise Missiles and NATO Missile Defense — Under the Radar?" Paris, France: Institut français des relations internationales (IFRI), Security Studies Centre, Spring 2012.

97. Schneider.

98. Renz and Thornton.

99. "*Soveshchaniye po vypolneniyu gosprogrammy vooruzheniya v oblasti yadernogo sderzhivaniya*" ("Conference on implementing the state armaments programme in the field of nuclear deterrence"), *Kremlin.ru*, July 26, 2012, available from *news.Kremlin.ru/news/16058*.

100. Frolov, Andrey. "Russian Military Spending in 2011-2020." Moscow Defense Brief, No. 1, 2011.

101. Dmitry Gorenburg, "Realities of Rearmament," Russian Defense Policy blog, June 22, 2012, available from *russiandefpolicy.wordpress.com/2012/06/22/realities-of-rearmament/*.

102. "The winner is . . .," *Russian Defense Policy*, March 9, 2012, available from *russiandefpolicy.wordpress.com/2012/03/09/the-winner-is/*.

103. "Defense news," *Russian Defense Policy*, April 25, 2012, available from *russiandefpolicy.wordpress.com/2012/04/25/defense-news-5/*.

104. "*Zakupki bronetekhniki prodolzhatsya, nesmotrya na slova Makarova*" ("Purchases of armoured vehicles will continue regardless of what Makarov says"), *RIA Novosti*, February 14, 2012, available from *ria.ru/defense_safety/20120214/565663330.html*.

105. "*Rogozin i Makarov posporili iz-za novogo bombardirovsh-chika*" ("Rogozin and Makarov argue over new bomber"), *Army News*, June 6, 2012, available from *army-news.ru/2012/06/rogozin-i-makarov-posporili-iz-za-novogo-bombardirovshhika/*.

106. "*Rogozin utochnil sroki nachala proizvodstva tankov na plat-forme 'Armata'*" ("Rogozin clarifies the timescale for beginning production of tanks on the Armata platform"), *RIA Novosti*, April 13, 2012.

107. "*Sovet dlya borby s monopolismom v sfere OPK sozdadut 29 iyunya – Rogozin*" ("A Council for Fighting Monopolism in the Defence Industrial Complex will be created on 29 June - Rogozin"), *RIA-Novosti*, June 28, 2012, available from *ria.ru/defense_safe-ty/20120628/686844070.html*.

108. Maya Mashatina, "Sukhoi Su-30SM: An Indian Gift to Russia's Air Force," *RIA Novosti*, March 23, 2012, available from *en.rian.ru/analysis/20120323/172357523.html*.

109. Anton Denisov, "Russia Announces 'Massive' Tank Scrappage Scheme," *RIA Novosti*, March 23, 2012, available from *en.rian.ru/mlitary_news/20120323/172346264.html*.

110. Mikhail Barabanov, "*Kriticheskii vzgliad na GPV-2020*" ("A critical look at the State Arms Program-2020"), *Voyenno-pro-myshlennyy kuryer*, January 8, 2013, available from *vpk-news.ru/articles/13870*.

111. Pallin, ed., p. 65 onwards.

112. Alexei Arbatov, "Real and Imaginary Threats: Military Power in World Politics in the 21st Century," *Russia in Global Af-fairs*, April 15, 2013, available from *carnegie.ru/2013/04/15/real-and-imaginary-threats/g0ms#*.

113. Ruslan Pukhov, "*Natsionalnaya oborona: vozmozhna eko-nomiya*" ("National Defence: Economies are Possible"), *Nezavi-simoye voyennoye obozreniye*, March 16, 2012, available from *nvo.ng.ru/forces/2012-03-16/11_economy.html*.

114. "Kudrin Stands Firm on Defense Spending During 'Timeout'," *The Moscow Times*, October 10, 2011.

115. Kira Latukhina, *"Lomat' stereotypy"* ("Breaking stereotype"), *Rossiyskaya Gazeta*, February 21, 2012.

116. *"Soveshchaniya po vypolneniyu gosudarstvennoy programmy v oblasti aviatsionnoy tekhniki"* ("Conference on Implementing the State Program for Aviation"), *Kremlin.ru*, June 14, 2012, available from *Kremlin.ru/transcripts/15646*.

117. Konstantin Bogdanov, *"Gosprogrammu vooruzheniya pridetsya perezagruzit' za tri goda"* ("State Program Will Have To Be Set Back Three Years"), *RIA-Novosti*, July 2, 2012, available from *www.ria.ru/analytics/20120702/690180731.html*.

118. *"Itogovyy otchet o rezul'tatakh dejatel'nosti ekspertnykh grupp po provedeniyu otsenki effektivnosti raskhodov federal'nogo bjudzheta i predstavleniyu predlozheniy po ikh optimiztsii"* ("Final report on the results of the activity of expert groups in carrying out an assessment of the effectiveness of expenditures of the Federal budget and presentation of recommendations on their optimisation"), Ministry of Finances of the Russian Federation website, September 3, 2009, available from *www1.minfin.ru/ru/?id56=19933*.

119. Aleksey Mikhaylov, *"Molodyye letchiki begut iz VVS"* ("Young Pilots Are Running From The Air Force"), *Izvestiya*, August 6, 2012, available from *izvestia.ru/news/531968*.

120. Arbatov and Dvorkin, p. 45.

121. Keir Giles, "Who Gives the Orders in the New Russian Military?" Rome, Italy: NATO Defense College, March 2012.

122. Viktor Litovkin, "VDV commander Shamanov interviewed on intermediate results of VDV reform," *Nezavisimoye voyennoye obozreniye*, March 2, 2012.

123. Vladimir Mukhin, *"Professionalnaya armiya poyavitsya cherez 100 let"* ("There will be a professional army in 100 years"), *Nezavisimoye voennoye obozreniye*, November 26, 2012, available from *www.ng.ru/printed/276089*.

124. Speaking at a briefing at NATO Defense College, Rome, Italy, November 27, 2012.

125. *Agentstvo voyennykh novostey*, May 23, 2012; *Rossiyskaya Gazeta*, May 29, 2012.

126. *Krasnaya Zvezda*, April 2, 2012, as cited in "OSC Report: Military Increases Officer Billets To Address Combat Readiness Problems," Reston, VA: Open Source Center, June 14, 2012.

127. Keir Giles, "Russia's Military Plans Versus Demographic Reality," Shrivenham, UK: Conflict Studies Research Centre, October 2006.

128. Mikhail Lukanin, "Demographics vs the Russian Army," Defense Brief, No 1, Moscow, Russia, 2011.

129. Aleksey Nikolskiy, *"Minoborony: nekomplekt v Vooruzhennykh silakh dostigayet 20%"* ("Ministry of Defence: Personnel deficit in Armed Forces reaches 20%"),*Vedomosti.ru*, June 9, 2012, available from *www.vedomosti.ru/politics/news/1837940/voennyh_ ne_hvataet#ixzz1ydVdnGXy*.

130. Author interviews with Russian officers who preferred to remain anonymous, late-2012.

131. Cimbala, "Russian Threat Perceptions and Security Policies: Soviet Shadows and Contemporary Challenges."

132. Pallin, ed., p. 104.

133. *"V VDV poyavyatsya mirotvorcheskiye batalyony"* ("Peacekeeping Battalions Will Make Their Appearance In The Airborne Assault Forces"), *Natsionalnaya oborona*, undated, available from *www.oborona.ru/pages/mainpage/news/index.shtml*.

134. Alexei Arbatov, "Real and Imaginary Threats: Military Power in World Politics in the 21st Century," *Russia in Global Affairs*, April 15, 2013, available from *carnegie.ru/2013/04/15/real-and-imaginary-threats/g0ms#*.

135. See, for example, *"Ucheniya na Kamchatke: rakety s krey-sera 'Varyag' ne doletali do tseli, boyevaya tekhnika zastrevala v peske"* ("Exercise in Kamchatka: missiles from the cruiser Varyag don't reach their target, military equipment stuck in the sand"), *Novyy region*, September 22, 2011, available from *nr2.ru/society/349713.html*; Igor Kravchuk, "Takogo pozora VMF RF eshche ne znal. Pokazushnyye ucheniya na Kamchatke" ("The Russian Navy has never seen such an embarrassment. Show exercise in Kamchatka"), *Gaidpark*, September 20, 2011, available from *gidepark.ru/user/2976644430/article/424394*.

136. Speaking at a briefing at NATO Defense College, Rome, Italy, November 27, 2012.

137. "Experiences and Conclusions of the Russian Military Exercises since 2009," in Forss, Kiianlinna, Inkkinen, and Hult, eds., *The Development of Russian Military Policy and Finland*.

138. Author interviews with Russian officers who preferred to remain anonymous, late-2012.

139. "Expanded meeting of the Defence Ministry Board," Russian presidential website, February 27, 2013, available from *eng.Kremlin.ru/transcripts/5050*.

140. See also Igor Korotchenko, *"Vooruzhennye sily Rossiyskoy Federatsii: modernizatsiya i perspektivy razvitiya"* ("Armed Forces of the Russian Federations: Modernisation and Prospects for Development"), *Natsionalnaya oborona*, 2012.

141. Giles, "Who Gives the Orders in the New Russian Military?"

142. Keir Giles, "Russian Operations in Georgia: Lessons Identified Versus Lessons Learned," in *The Russian Armed Forces in Transition*.

143. Frederic Labarre, "Defence Innovation and Russian Foreign Policy," J. Larry Black, ed., *Russia after 2012*, New York: Routledge, 2012.

144. Pallin, ed., "Russian Military Capability in a Ten-Year Perspective—2011," p. 21.

145. "Russia—Future Directions," Shrivenham, UK: Advanced Research and Assessment Group, Defence Academy of the United Kingdom, October 1, 2008. See also Labarre.

www.ingramcontent.com/pod-product-compliance
Lightning Source LLC
Chambersburg PA
CBHW071113280526
45787CB00003B/1026